The Lucky

Reference Book

SCHOLASTIC BOOK CLUBS

SCHOLASTIC INC.
New York Toronto London Auckland Sydney
Mexico City New Delhi Hong Kong

ISBN 0-439-13224-X

Cover design by Karen Hudson. Interior by Louise Bova

12 11 10 9 8 7 6 5 4 3 2 1 9/9 0 1 2 3 4/0

Printed in the U.S.A. 01

First Scholastic printing, September 1999

Table of Contents

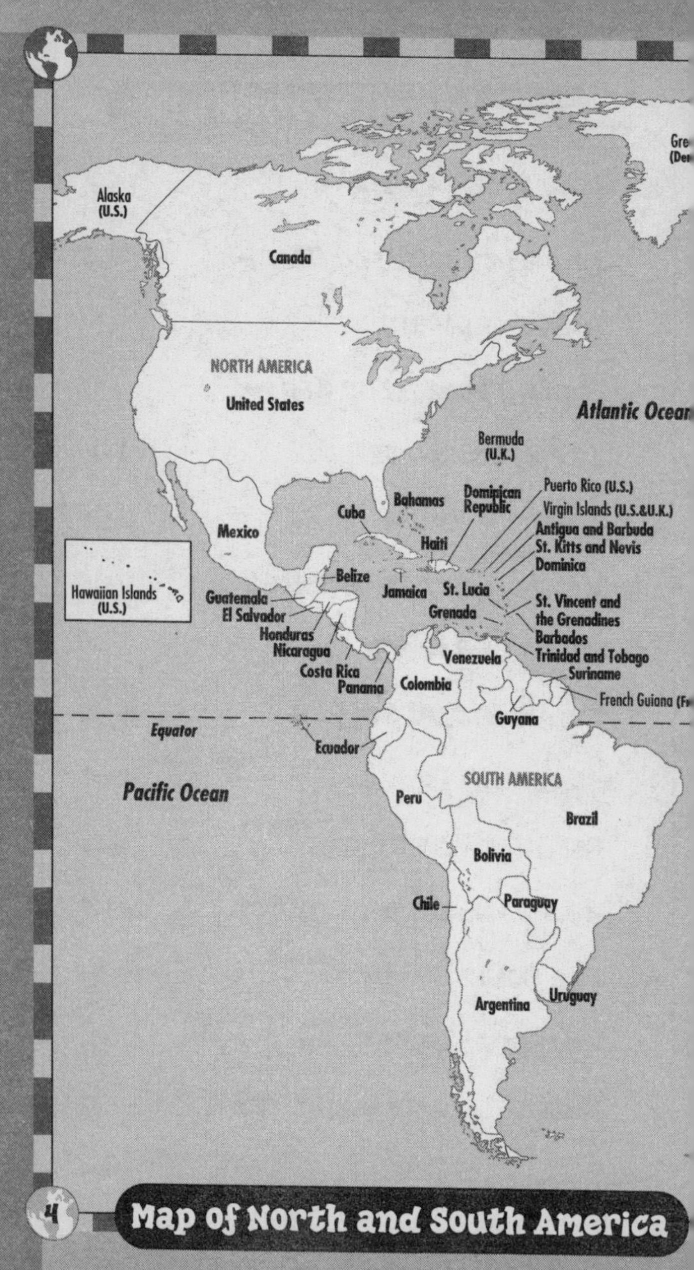

Map of North and South America

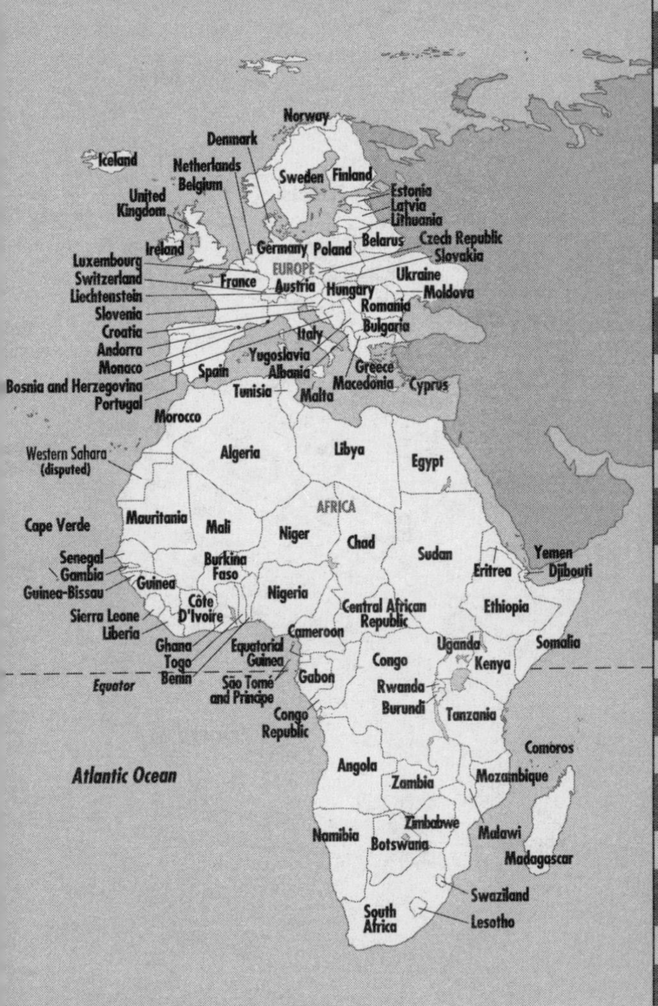

Map of Africa and Europe

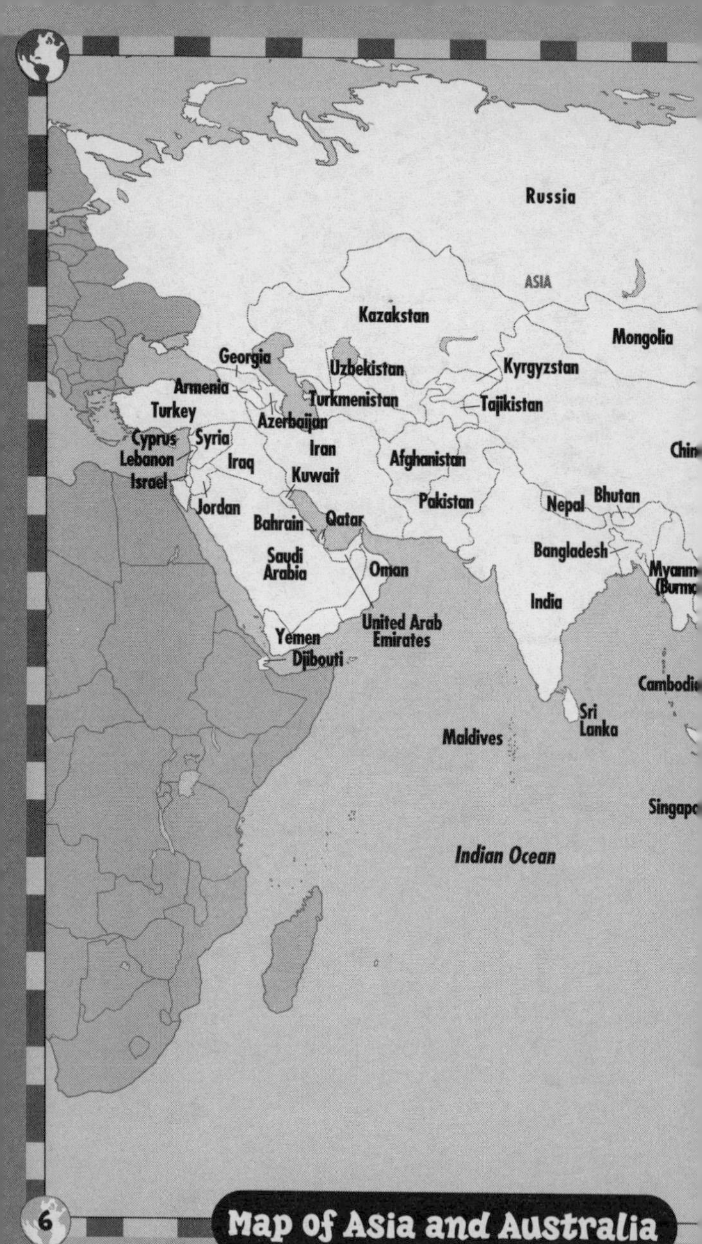
Russia
ASIA
Kazakstan
Mongolia
Georgia
Uzbekistan
Kyrgyzstan
Armenia
Turkmenistan
Tajikistan
Turkey
Azerbaijan
Cyprus
Syria
Lebanon
Israel
Iraq
Iran
Afghanistan
Kuwait
Jordan
Pakistan
Nepal
Bhutan
Bahrain
Qatar
Bangladesh
Saudi Arabia
Oman
India
United Arab Emirates
Yemen
Djibouti
Sri Lanka
Maldives
Indian Ocean
Map of Asia and Australia

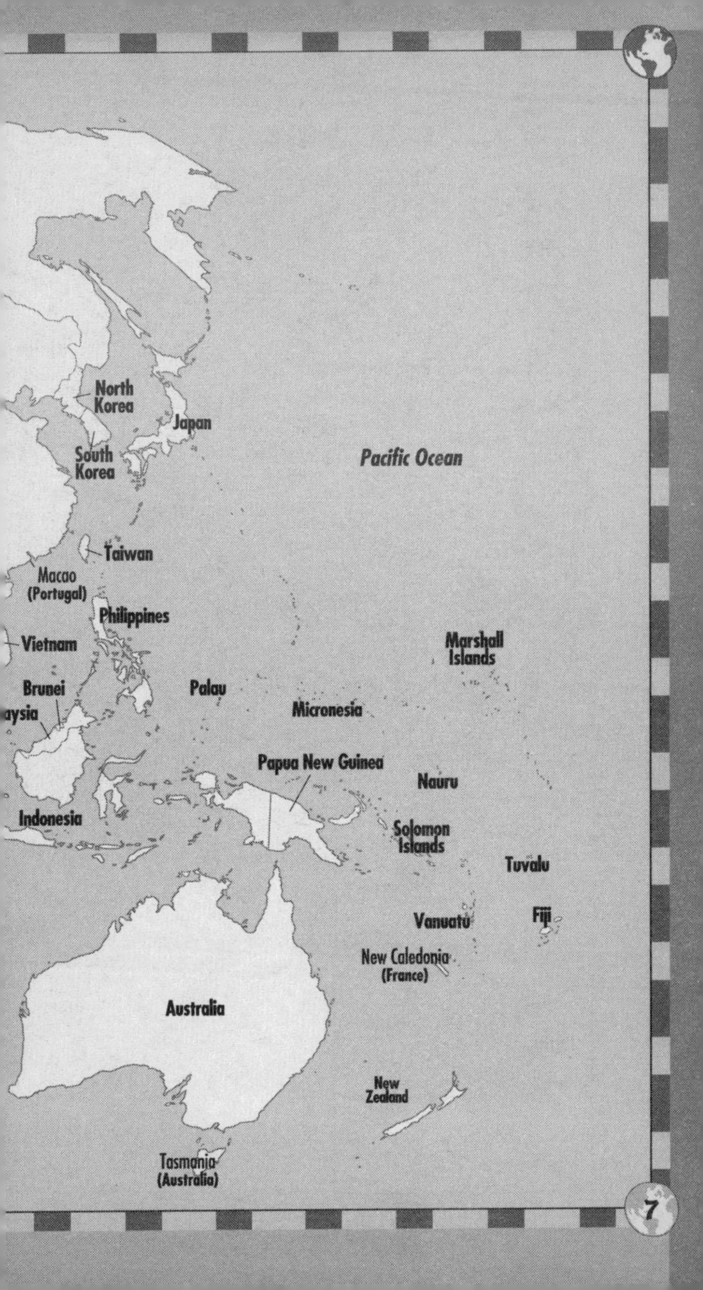
North Korea
Japan
South Korea
Pacific Ocean
Taiwan
Macao (Portugal)
Philippines
Vietnam
Marshall Islands
Brunei
Palau
aysia
Micronesia
Papua New Guinea
Nauru
Indonesia
Solomon Islands
Tuvalu
Vanuatu
Fiji
New Caledonia (France)
Australia
New Zealand
Tasmania (Australia)

Vancouver
Calgary
Victoria
Regina
Seattle
Tacoma
Spokane
WA
Portland
Salem
Eugene
OR
Helena
MT
Butte
Bismarck
Billings
Boise
ID
Idaho Falls
Sheridan
SD
Rapid City
WY
Ogden
Salt Lake City
Provo
UT
Reno
Sacramento
Oakland
San Francisco
NV
Cheyenne
NE
Boulder
Denver
Colorado Springs
CO
Pueblo
Fresno
CA
Bakersfield
Las Vegas
Santa Barbara
Los Angeles
Long Beach
San Diego
Mexicali
Pacific Ocean
AZ
Phoenix
Tucson
Santa Fe
Albuquerque
NM
Roswell
El Paso
Amarillo
San Angelo
Hermosillo
Chihuahua
Honolulu
Hawaii
Nuevo Laredo
Monterrey
Culiacan
Durango
Ciudad Victoria
MEXICO
San Luis Potosi
Guadalajara
Mexico City
Colima
Anchorage
Juneau
Alaska

Map of the United States

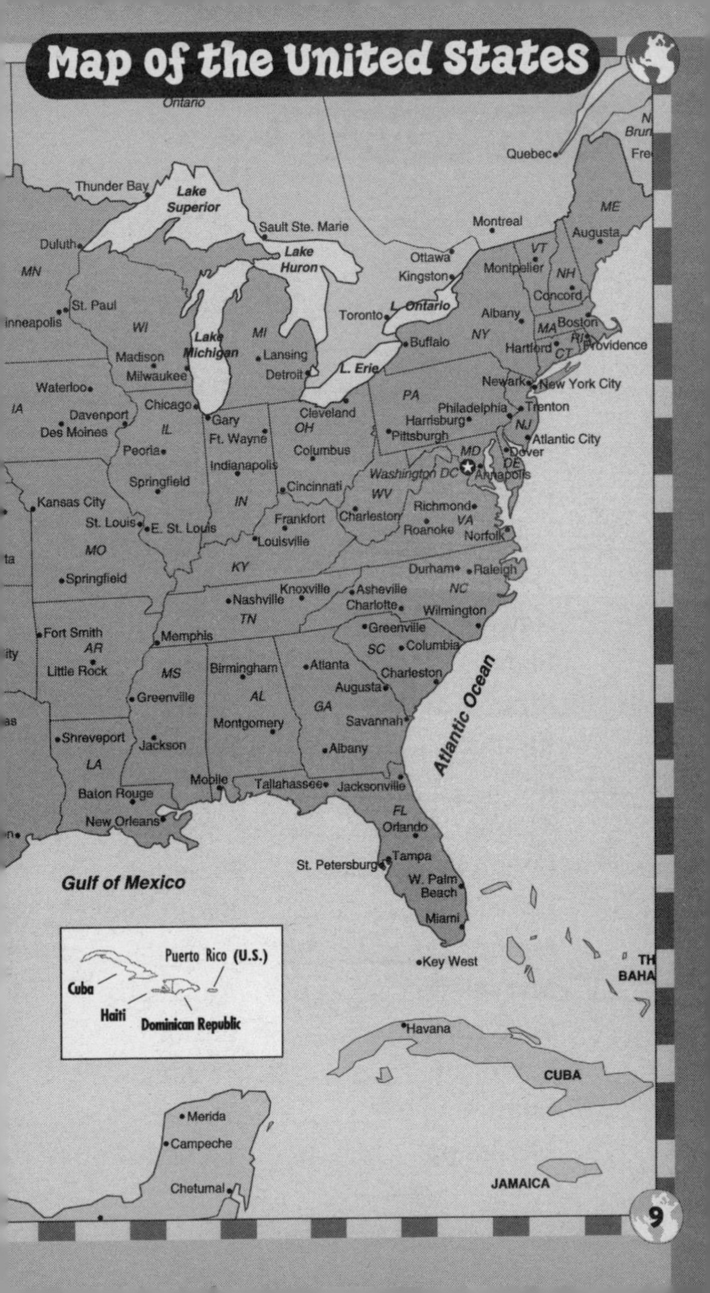

State Capitals

Alabama	→	Montgomery
Alaska	→	Juneau
Arizona	→	Phoenix
Arkansas	→	Little Rock
California	→	Sacramento
Colorado	→	Denver
Connecticut	→	Hartford
Delaware	→	Dover
Florida	→	Tallahassee
Georgia	→	Atlanta
Hawaii	→	Honolulu
Idaho	→	Boise
Illinois	→	Springfield
Indiana	→	Indianapolis
Iowa	→	Des Moines
Kansas	→	Topeka
Kentucky	→	Frankfort
Louisiana	→	Baton Rouge
Maine	→	Augusta
Maryland	→	Annapolis
Massachusetts	→	Boston
Michigan	→	Lansing
Minnesota	→	St. Paul
Mississippi	→	Jackson

Missouri →	Jefferson City
Montana →	Helena
Nebraska →	Lincoln
Nevada →	Carson City
New Hampshire →	Concord
New Jersey →	Trenton
New Mexico →	Santa Fe
New York →	Albany
North Carolina →	Raleigh
North Dakota →	Bismarck
Ohio →	Columbus
Oklahoma →	Oklahoma City
Oregon →	Salem
Pennsylvania →	Harrisburg
Rhode Island →	Providence
South Carolina →	Columbia
South Dakota →	Pierre
Tennessee →	Nashville
Texas →	Austin
Utah →	Salt Lake City
Vermont →	Montpelier
Virginia →	Richmond
Washington →	Olympia
West Virginia →	Charleston
Wisconsin →	Madison
Wyoming →	Cheyenne

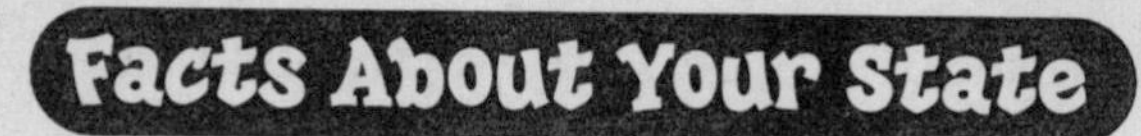

Facts About Your State

Name of State ______________________

Abbreviation of State's Name ______________

Nickname of State ____________________

Date Admitted to the United States _________

Governor ______________________

Population ______________________

State Flower ______________________

State Bird ______________________

State Tree ______________________

State Song ______________________

Famous Places in the State

____

____

____

____

____

Saying on State's License Plate

____

President	Dates of Term(s)
1. George Washington	April 30, 1789–March 3, 1797
2. John Adams	March 4, 1797–March 3, 1801
3. Thomas Jefferson	March 4, 1801–March 3, 1809
4. James Madison	March 4, 1809–March 3, 1817
5. James Monroe	March 4, 1817–March 3, 1825
6. John Quincy Adams	March 4, 1825–March 3, 1829
7. Andrew Jackson	March 4, 1829–March 3, 1837
8. Martin Van Buren	March 4, 1837–March 3, 1841
9. William Henry Harrison	March 4, 1841–April 4, 1841*
10. John Tyler	April 6, 1841–March 3, 1845
11. James Knox Polk	March 4, 1845–March 3, 1849
12. Zachary Taylor	March 4, 1849–July 9, 1850*
13. Millard Fillmore	July 10, 1850–March 3, 1853
14. Franklin Pierce	March 4, 1853–March 3, 1857
15. James Buchanan	March 4, 1857–March 3, 1861
16. Abraham Lincoln	March 4, 1861–April 15, 1865*
17. Andrew Johnson	April 15, 1865–March 3, 1869
18. Ulysses Simpson Grant	March 4, 1869–March 3, 1877
19. Rutherford Birchard Hayes	March 4, 1877–March 3, 1881
20. James Abram Garfield	March 4, 1881–Sept. 19, 1881*
21. Chester Alan Arthur	Sept. 20, 1881–March 3, 1885

22. Grover Cleveland	March 4, 1885–March 3, 1889
23. Benjamin Harrison	March 4, 1889–March 3, 1893
24. Grover Cleveland	March 4, 1893–March 3, 1897
25. William McKinley	March 4, 1897–Sept. 14, 1901*
26. Theodore Roosevelt	Sept. 14, 1901–March 3, 1909
27. William Howard Taft	March 4, 1909–March 3, 1913
28. Woodrow Wilson	March 4, 1913–March 3, 1921
29. Warren Gamaliel Harding	March 4, 1921–Aug. 2, 1923*
30. Calvin Coolidge	Aug. 3, 1923–March 3, 1929
31. Herbert Clark Hoover	March 4, 1929–March 3, 1933
32. Franklin Delano Roosevelt	March 4, 1933–April 12, 1945*
33. Harry S. Truman	April 12, 1945–Jan. 20, 1953
34. Dwight David Eisenhower	Jan. 20, 1953–Jan. 20, 1961
35. John Fitzgerald Kennedy	Jan. 20, 1961–Nov. 22, 1963*
36. Lyndon Baines Johnson	Nov. 22, 1963–Jan. 20, 1969
37. Richard Milhous Nixon	Jan. 20, 1969–Aug. 9, 1974**
38. Gerald Rudolph Ford	Aug. 9, 1974–Jan. 20, 1977
39. James Earl Carter, Jr.	Jan. 20, 1977–Jan. 20, 1981
40. Ronald Wilson Reagan	Jan. 20, 1981–Jan. 20, 1989
41. George Herbert Walker Bush	Jan. 20, 1989–Jan. 20, 1993
42. William Jefferson Clinton	Jan. 20, 1993–

*Died while in office

**Resigned from office

Spelling Rules

To Double or Not to Double

Some words end with one consonant that follows a short vowel sound.

Double the final consonant before you add an ending that begins with a vowel.

step+ing=stepping
step+ed=stepped

hot+est=hottest
swim+er=swimmer
sun+y=sunny

Do not double the final consonant when you add an ending that begins with a consonant.

glad+ly=gladly

The Last Word on Final *e*

Some words end with a consonant and a silent **e**.

Drop the final **e** before you add an ending that begins with a vowel.

use+ing=using
share+ed=shared

Don't drop the final **e** before you add an ending that begins with a consonant.

like+ly=likely pave+ment=pavement

The Final *y* Rule

Some verbs end in **y**.
Change the **y** to **i** before you add **ed**.
Don't change the spelling when you add **ing**.

dry+ed=dried carry+ed=carried
dry+ing=drying carry+ing=carrying

The *i–e* Rule to Believe

The rules in this rhyme work most of the time:

Put **i** before **e** except after **c** or when the sound is an **a** as in neighbor and weigh.

Put *i* before *e*	Except after *c*	Exceptions
pie	ceiling	either
tie	receive	height
achieve		their
believe	**Sounds like long *a***	weird
chief	neighbor	
niece	reindeer	
piece	weigh	
field	weight	
	eight	

Words Often Misspelled

about
afraid
afternoon
always
anyone
anyway
because
before
blue
children
come
could
does
done
down
easy
eight
every
everyone
father
first
four
friend
from
gone
good

have
hello
high
how
inside
into
just
live
loose
lose
love
many
might
money
most
mother
much
name
new
nice
none
now
off
once
one
our

out
outside
play
pretty
put
right
said
Saturday
saw
school
send
shoes
should
show
some
sometimes
soon
Sunday
sure
talk
than
that
them
then
there
these
think
this
time
today
together
too
two
upon
use
very
was
Wednesday
were
what
when
where
which
while
white
who
whole
whose
with
woman
women
would
write

Parts of Speech

A **noun** is a word that names a person, a place, or a thing. Nouns can also name feelings and ideas.

A **pronoun** is a word that can take the place of a noun.

A **verb** is a word that tells about an action. Some verbs tell about actions that are happening now. These verbs are in the **present tense**. Some verbs name actions that happened in the past. These verbs are in the **past tense.**

An **adjective** is a word that tells more about the noun. Adjectives may describe number, color, or size. Adjectives may describe how something looks or sounds. Adjectives may describe how something tastes, feels, or smells.

An **adverb** is a word that tells more about the verb. Some adverbs tell **how**. Some adverbs tell **when** or **where**.

Prefixes and Suffixes

Prefixes and **suffixes** are word parts that can be added to words. A prefix is added at the beginning of a word. A suffix is added to the ending of a word. When a prefix or suffix is added to a word, that word's meaning is changed.

The prefix *un-* makes the base word mean its opposite.

unhappy
unfair
unequal
uncover
unbutton
unzip

The prefix *auto-* means "self."

autograph
automobile
autobiography
automatic

The prefix *re-* adds "again" to a word's meaning.

retell
rewrite
reuse
recycle
reheat
review

The prefix *tele-* means "far away" or "from a distance."

television
telegram
telescope
telephone

The suffix *-ful* **changes a word. It adds the meaning "full" to the word.**

careful
tearful
helpful
colorful
beautiful
cheerful

The suffix *-ly* **adds the meaning "like" to the word.**

slowly
nicely
evenly
softly
quietly
happily

The suffix *-er* **sometimes adds the meaning "a person who does" to a word.**

singer
teacher
reader
painter
seller
pitcher

The suffix *-er* **sometimes adds the meaning "more" to a word.**

smaller
softer
faster
taller
slower
higher

Sounding It Out

Below you will find an easy way to figure out how to pronounce a new word. By joining the sounds of a new word together, you'll be able to pronounce it properly. This will allow you to pronounce words in one way, although some words are pronounced differently depending on what part of the country you live in.

Vowels

a	as in	m**a**d, p**a**t
ah	as in	f**a**ther
air	as in	f**air**, c**are**
ar	as in	d**ar**k
ay	as in	p**ay**, accl**ai**m
aw	as in	r**aw**, c**au**ght
e	as in	m**e**t, m**e**n
ee	as in	b**ee**t
i	as in	b**i**t, acc**i**dent
ihr	as in	f**ear**, h**ere**
eye	as in	**i**ron, rabb**i**
o	as in	c**o**t, d**o**t
oh	as in	f**oe**, d**ou**gh
oo	as in	p**oo**l, r**u**de
or	as in	c**or**n, m**ore**
oi	as in	b**oi**l, t**oy**
ou	as in	h**ow**, **ou**ch
u	as in	p**u**t, b**oo**k
uh	as in	b**u**n, nat**io**n, comm**a**

ur	as in	b**ur**n, wo**rk**e**r**
yoo	as in	m**u**sic, p**ure**

Consonants

b	as in	**b**ad, so**b**
ch	as in	**ch**ip, dit**ch**
d	as in	**d**ip, re**d**
f	as in	**f**un, cu**ff**, lau**gh**
g	as in	**g**et, be**g**
h	as in	**h**am
j	as in	**j**am, ed**ge**
k	as in	**k**eep, sa**ck**
l	as in	**l**ap, te**ll**
m	as in	**m**an, la**mb**
n	as in	**n**ow, te**n**, **gn**at, **kn**ow
ng	as in	si**ng**
p	as in	**p**an, si**p**
r	as in	**r**ib, pou**r**
s	as in	**s**et
ss	as in	mi**ss**, ra**ce**, ye**s**
sh	as in	**sh**ip, ra**sh**
t	as in	**t**ub, ra**t**
th	as in	**th**in, ba**th**
TH	as in	**th**is, ba**the**
v	as in	**v**an, hi**ve**
w	as in	**w**ell, **wh**ale
y	as in	**y**ell
z	as in	**z**ip, ha**s**, tho**se**
zh	as in	mea**s**ure

Familiar Homonyms

Words that sound the same but have diffe
meanings and different spellings

ant/aunt
The **ant** is a frequent visitor at picnics.
My **aunt** is my father's sister.

ate/eight
I **ate** lunch at school last week.
I have **eight** video games.

berry/bury
The **berry** from that bush is poisonous.
The squirrel tried to **bury** the acorn.

blew/blue
The storm **blew** in from the west.
Blue is my favorite color.

brake/break
I had to **brake** to slow down my bicycle.
I didn't mean to **break** the glass vase.

cent/scent/sent
I don't have a **cent** to my name!
That perfume has an awful **scent**.
I **sent** a letter to my best friend.

dear/deer
My puppy is very **dear** to me.
I saw some **deer** at the petting zoo.

fair/fare
The weather is **fair** today.
I paid full **fare** for my airplane ticket.

hear/here
Please speak louder because I can't **hear** you.
Come over **here**!

hole/whole
My dog dug a **hole** in the backyard.
I read the **whole** book in one morning.

hour/our
I'll be ready in one **hour**.
Our next meeting is in one month.

know/no
I didn't **know** half the answers on the quiz.
No, I don't think I passed.

meat/meet
I'm a vegetarian now, so I don't eat **meat**.
Meet me at the mall at seven o'clock.

one/won
Give me **one** good reason for going to study hall.

Our team **won** at the science fair.

pair/pear

I have one **pair** of jeans.
The apple looks tastier than the **pear**.

plain/plane

The skirt was **plain**, but the blouse was fancy.
We flew on a **plane** to visit my grandfather.

pray/prey

Let's **pray** for good weather for our field trip.
Eagles and owls are birds of **prey**.

right/write

Turn **right** at the corner.
Write a letter to your uncle.

role/roll

I auditioned for a **role** in the school play.
My favorite lunch is peanut butter and jelly on a **roll**.

scene/seen

She painted a forest **scene** in art class.
I haven't **seen** her since three o'clock.

some/sum

Have **some** pie if you're hungry.
The **sum** of two and two is four.

son/sun

The father had one **son** and three daughters.
The **sun** rises in the east.

tail/tale

My dog has a very long **tail**.
Did you read the **tale** of Paul Bunyan and Babe, the blue ox?

their/there/they're

Their house is on the next block.
Her dog is **there**, behind the fence.
They're going to be happy after the quiz.

threw/through

She **threw** the ball past home plate.
The ball flew **through** the air.

to/too/two

I went **to** the dance.
My friend came, **too**.
The **two** of us danced together.

way/weigh

Let's take the back **way** home.
How many pounds do you **weigh**?

weak/week

She grew thin and **weak** from her illness.
It took one **week** to recover.

wear/where

I thought I'd **wear** cutoffs to camp.
Where did I put my homework?

which/witch

Which witch is **which**?
The **witch** knew hundreds of spells.

How to Use a Dictionary

Guide Words usually appear in the outer corner of each page of a dictionary. The first guide word identifies the first main entry on the page. The second word identifies the last word on the page.

Main entry word or words are usually set in bold type.

Word divisions are shown in the main entry for words of two or more syllables.

Parts of speech are identified for each main entry or subentry.

Definitions of the main entry follow the listing of pronunciation and part of speech. Definitions tell the meaning of the main entry.

radio —rain

ra•di•o (**ray**-dee-oh)

1. NOUN A piece of equipment that you use to listen to sounds sent by electrical waves.

2. ADJECTIVE **radio**

3. VERB To send a message using a radio.

VERB **radioing, radioed**

Pronunciation of the main entry follows the entry word or words.

Illustrations are used to add visual reinforcements to written definitions.

Multiple definitions are provided for words with more than one meaning.

The Solar System

The Planets in Order of Size

(from smallest to largest)

Pluto
Mercury
Mars
Venus
Earth
Neptune
Uranus
Saturn
Jupiter

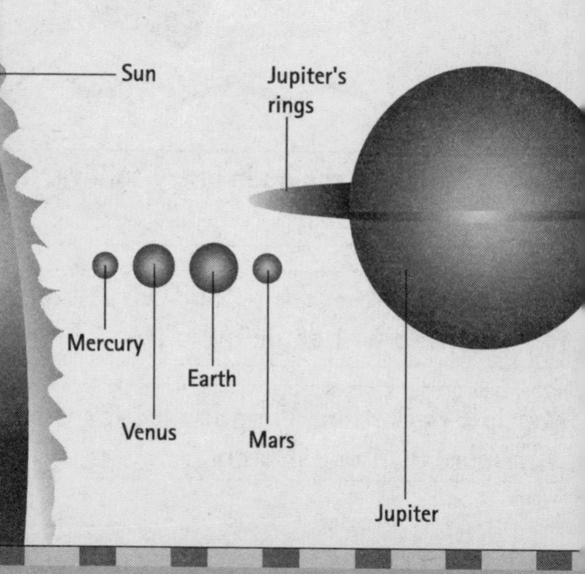

Planets' Distance from the Sun

Mercury →	35,980,000 miles
Venus →	67,230,000 miles
Earth →	92,960,000 miles
Mars →	141,000,000 miles
Jupiter →	483,600,000 miles
Saturn →	888,222,000 miles
Uranus →	1,786,400,000 miles
Neptune →	2,798,800,000 miles
Pluto →	3,666,200,000 miles

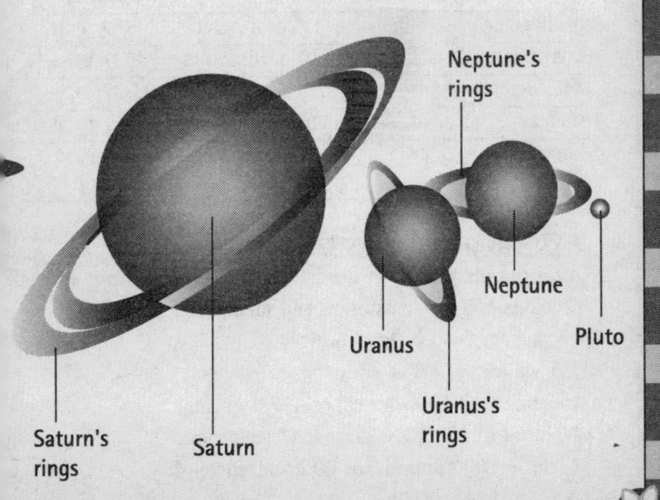

Measurements

The **U.S. Customary System**, also called the **English System**, is our standard for measuring length. The system is a combination of a number of ancient measures. It is used along with the **metric system.**

U.S. Customary Measures of Length

Measure	Abbreviation	Equivalent
inch	in.	1/12 foot
foot	ft.	12 inches
yard	yd.	3 feet (36 inches)
mile	mi.	1,760 yards (5,280 feet)

Metric	Abbreviation	Length	U.S. Equivalents (Rounded)
millimeter	mm	.1 centimeter	.0393 inch
centimeter	cm	10 millimeters	.3937 inch
decimeter	dm	10 centimeters	3.937 inches
meter	m	100 centimeters	39.37 inches
kilometer	km	1000 meters	1,093 yards (.6 mile)

Avoirdupois Weight

Avoirdupois weight is used to measure everything except precious metals, gemstones, and medicine.

1 grain (gr.) = 0.002285 ounces

1 dram (dr.) = 27.34 grains

1 ounce (oz.) = 16 drams, or 437.5 grains

1 pound (lb.) = 7,000 grains, or 16 ounces

1 ton = 2,000 pounds, or 20 hundredweights

Metric and U.S. Customary Weight Equivalents

Metric	Abbreviation	Metric Equivalent	U.S. Customary Equivalent
gram	g	1,000 milligrams	.0353 ounce
milligram	mg	.001 gram	.0154 grains
centigram	cg	10 milligrams	.154 grains
kilogram	kg	1,000 grams	2.204 pounds

Metric Volume Measures

10 milliliters (ml) = 1 centiliter (cl)

10 centiliters = 1 deciliter (dl) = 100 milliliters

10 deciliters = 1 liter (l) = 1,000 milliliters

1 liter(s) = 10 deciliter (dl) = 100 centiliters

U.S. Customary Liquid Volume Measures

Measure	Abbreviation	Equivalent
cup	c	8 ounces
pint	pt.	2 cups
quart	qt.	2 pints
gallon	gal.	4 quarts

Multiplication Facts Table

It's important to know multiplication facts. You ca
use a multiplication facts table like this to find th
product of any multiplication from 0 x 0 to 9 x 9. Th
bold numbers are factors. All the other numbers ar
products.

X	**0**	**1**	**2**	**3**	**4**	**5**	**6**	**7**	**8**	**9**
0	0	0	0	0	0	0	0	0	0	0
1	0	1	2	3	4	5	6	7	8	9
2	0	2	4	6	8	10	12	14	16	18
3	0	3	6	9	12	15	18	21	24	27
4	0	4	8	12	16	20	24	28	32	36
5	0	5	10	15	20	25	30	35	40	45
6	0	6	12	18	24	30	36	42	48	54
7	0	7	14	21	28	35	42	49	56	63
8	0	8	16	24	32	40	48	56	64	72
9	0	9	18	27	36	45	54	63	72	81

REMEMBER! *Examples:*

If you multiply any number by 0, the product is 0.
0 x 4 = 0 0 x 9 = 0
If you multiply any number by 1, the product is
that number. 1 x 5 = 5
If you change the order of the factors, the product
is the same. 6 x 7 = 42 7 x 6 = 42